TABLE OF CONTENTS

Vermont 3
Glossary 22
Index 24

A Crabtree Seedlings Book

Crabtree Publishing
crabtreebooks.com

School-to-Home Support for Caregivers and Teachers

This book helps children grow by letting them practice reading. Here are a few guiding questions to help the reader build his or her comprehension skills. Possible answers appear in red.

Before Reading:

- What do I know about Vermont?
    - *I know that Vermont is a state.*
    - *I know that Vermont is known for its maple syrup.*

- What do I want to learn about Vermont?
    - *I want to learn which famous people were born in Vermont.*
    - *I want to learn what the state flag looks like.*

During Reading:

- What have I learned so far?
    - *I have learned that Montpelier is the state capital of Vermont.*
    - *I have learned that Ben & Jerry's ice cream factory was originally going to make bagels.*

- I wonder why...
    - *I wonder why the state flower is the red clover.*
    - *I wonder why Vermont makes so much maple syrup.*

After Reading:

- What did I learn about Vermont?
    - *I have learned that you can ride in paddleboats at Emerald Lake State Park.*
    - *I have learned that the state animal is the Morgan horse.*

- Read the book again and look for the glossary words.
    - *I see the word* ***capital*** *on page 6, and the word* ***factory*** *on page 15. The other glossary words are found on pages 22 and 23.*

VERMONT
Hi! My name is Charlotte. Welcome to Vermont!

I live in Shelburne. It is along the **shore** of Lake Champlain.

The Shelburne Museum has many **historic** buildings. Each building has something interesting to see!

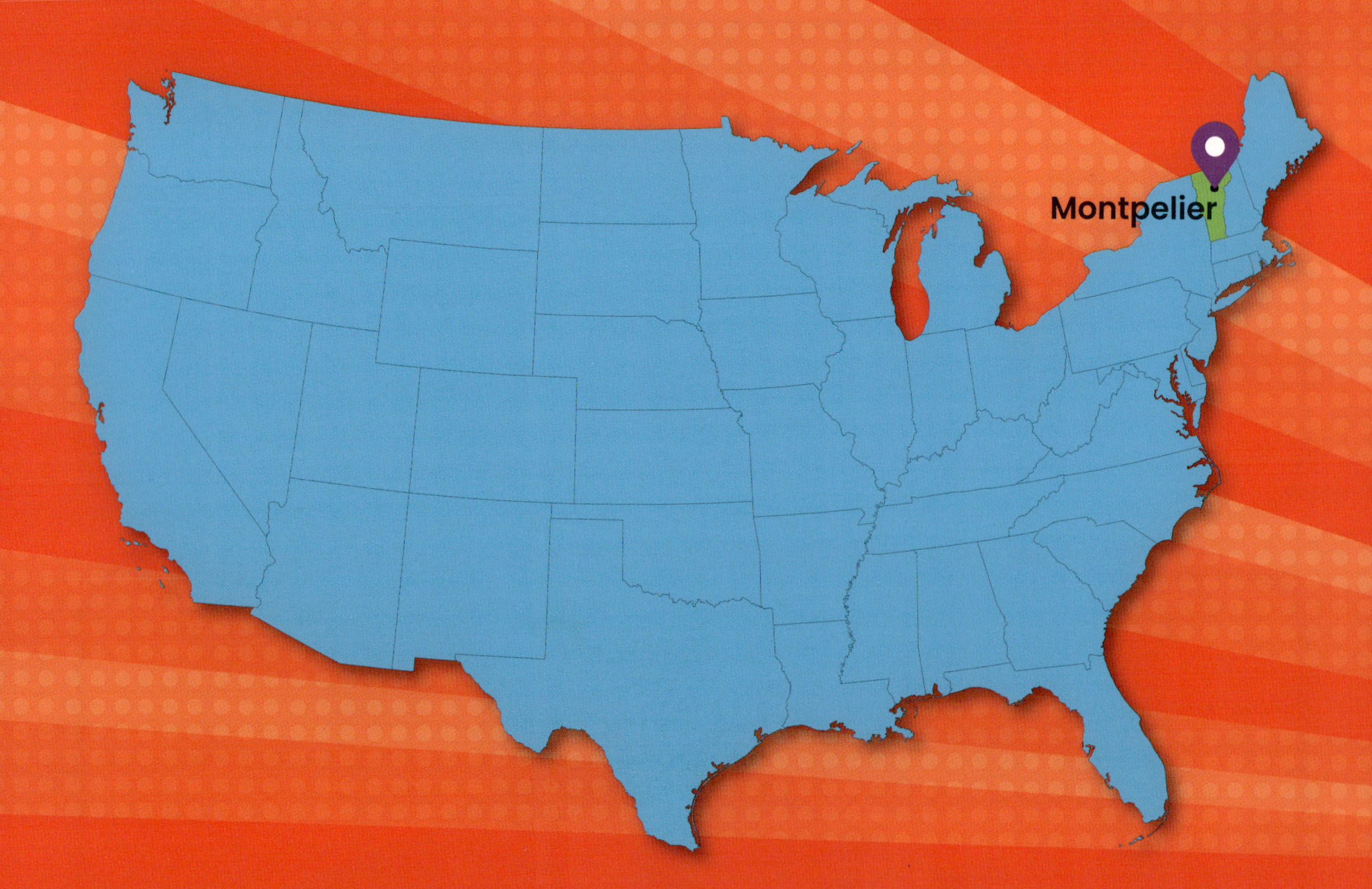

Vermont is in the northeastern United States. The **capital** is Montpelier.

Fun Fact: Burlington is the largest city in Vermont.

The state animal is the Morgan horse.

The red clover is the state flower.

We make a lot of maple syrup in Vermont. Most of it is used for pancakes.

Fun Fact: Vermont makes more than 2 million gallons (7.5 million liters) of maple syrup a year.

My state flag is blue. The state **coat of arms** is in the middle.

My family and I like to watch the Vermont Lake Monsters play baseball.

Fun Fact: The factory was originally going to make bagels.

I like to visit Ben & Jerry's ice cream factory. It is fun to try the different flavors.
BEN&JERRY'S
FACTORY TOURS

My family and I like to go hiking at Quechee State Park. The **gorge** at the park is beautiful!

Riding in a paddleboat at Emerald Lake State Park is relaxing.

Voice actress Susan Bennett, the original voice of Siri, was born in Vermont. Olympic snowboarding champion Ross Powers was also born in Vermont.

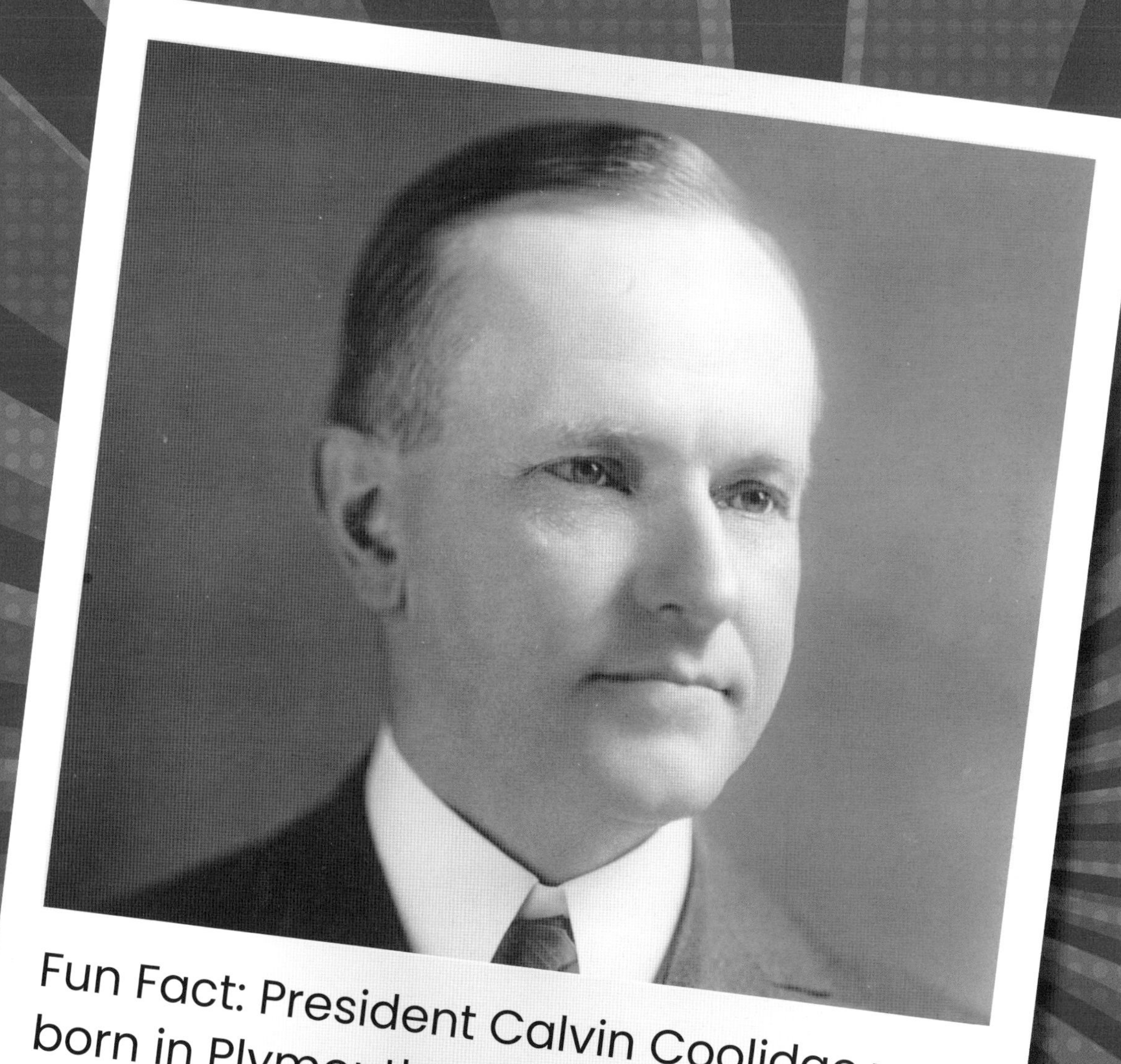

Fun Fact: President Calvin Coolidge was born in Plymouth, Vermont.

I like to swim in the Norcross-West Marble Quarry.

I enjoy skiing at Killington Ski Resort.

Glossary

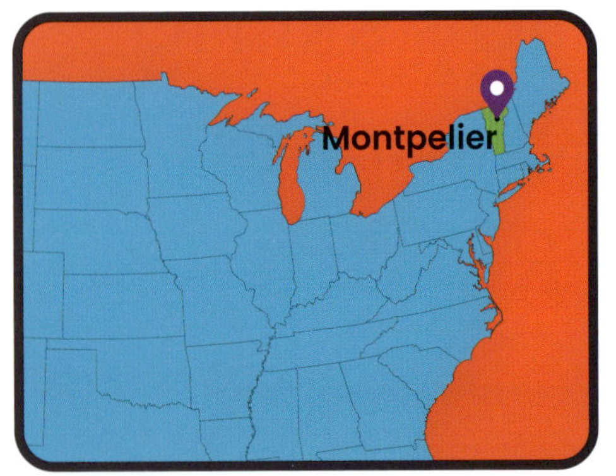

capital (cap-ih-tuhl): The city or town where the government of a country, state, or province is located

coat of arms (coht uv armz): A special group of pictures, usually shown on a shield

factory (fak-tor-ee): A building where machines are used to make things

gorge (gorj): A narrow valley between hills or mountains

historic (hi-stor-ik): Something that is important in history

shore (shor): The land along the edge of a body of water

Index

Coolidge, Calvin 19

maple syrup 10, 11

Quechee State Park 16

Shelburne 4, 5

skiing 21

Vermont Lake Monsters 13

About the Author

Christina Earley lives in sunny South Florida with her husband and son. She enjoys traveling around the United States and learning about different historical places. Her hobbies include hiking, yoga, and baking.

Written by: Christina Earley

Designed and Illustrated by: Bobbie Houser

Series Development: James Earley

Proofreader: Melissa Boyce

Educational Consultant: Marie Lemke M.Ed.

Photographs:
Alamy: Ian Dagnall: p. 14-15, 22; Tibbut Archive: p. 18 left; JIM BOURG/REUTERS: p. 18 righ; Jorge Tutor: p. 20
LOC: p. 19
Newscom: Ed Wolfstein/Icon SMI 756: p. 13
Shutterstock: Sean Pavone: cover, p. 7; Stock for you: p. 3; vermontalm: p. 4, 23; Harold Stiver: p. 5, 23; Volina: p. 6, 22; Lisa Kolbenschlag: p. 8; Grigorii Pisotsckii: p. 9; meunierd: p. 10-11; Andrew Cline: p. 11; Millenius: p. 12, 22; littlenySTOCK: p. 14; Gabe Shakour: p. 16, 23; trsers: p. 17; Outlook: p. 21

Crabtree Publishing

crabtreebooks.com 800-387-7650

Printed in the U.S.A./072023/CG20230214

Published in Canada
Crabtree Publishing
616 Welland Avenue
St. Catharines, Ontario
L2M 5V6

Published in the United States
Crabtree Publishing
347 Fifth Avenue
Suite 1402-145
New York, New York, 10016

Library and Archives Canada Cataloguing in Publication
Available at Library and Archives Canada

Library of Congress Cataloging-in-Publication Data
Available at the Library of Congress

Hardcover: 978-1-0398-0538-5
Paperback: 978-1-0398-0570-5
Ebook (pdf): 978-1-0398-0634-4
Epub: 978-1-0398-0602-3